Superstar Cars

Bugatti

Molly Aloian

Crabtree Publishing Company

www.crabtreebooks.com

Superstar Cars

Author: Molly Aloian
Publishing plan research and development:
   Sean Charlebois, Reagan Miller
   Crabtree Publishing Company
Editors: Sonya Newland, Adrianna Morganelli
Proofreader: Wendy Scavuzzo
Editorial director: Kathy Middleton
Project coordinator and prepress technician: Ken Wright
Print coordinator: Katherine Berti
Series consultant: Petrina Gentile
Cover design: Ken Wright
Design: Simon Borrough
Photo research: Sonya Newland

Produced for Crabtree Publishing by
White-Thomson Publishing

Photographs:
Alamy: Les. Ladbury: p. 36; Ian Shipley SP: p. 39; **Corbis:** Bruno de Hogues/Sygma: pp. 28-29; Swim Ink 2, LLC: p. 30; Martyn Goddard: pp. 34-35, 46-47, 47; Thierry Orban/Sygma: pp. 48, 48-49; **Flickr/Creative Commons License:** Ed Callow: p. 9; Exfordy: pp. 10, 33; El Caganer: p. 22; Sicnag: pp. 24-25; Bildmaschine: pp. 26-27; Aresauburn: p. 45; **Getty Images:** Gamma-Rapho: pp. 18, 34, 44, 50-51; Time & Life Pictures: pp. 40-41; **Motoring Picture Library:** pp. 1, 6-7, 11, 13, 14, 15, 16-17, 18-19, 20, 21, 23, 24, 38-39, 52-53, 53; **Shutterstock:** Gustavo Fadel: cover (car); Christoff: pp. 4-5; Sam Moores: pp. 7, 56; Max Earey: pp. 8-9, 56-57; Roberto Cerruti: pp. 26, 31; siraphat: p. 32; ENCKOphotography: 54-55, 58-59; **Thinkstock:** cover (background); **Topfoto:** Roger-Viollet: p. 42; **Wikipedia:** AlfvanBeem: p. 37; MPW57: pp. 42-43.

Library and Archives Canada Cataloguing in Publication

Aloian, Molly
     Bugatti / Molly Aloian.

(Superstar cars)
Includes index.
Issued also in electronic formats.
ISBN 978-0-7787-2100-0 (bound).--ISBN 978-0-7787-2105-5 (pbk.)

     1. Bugatti automobile--Juvenile literature.
I. Title. II. Series: Superstar cars

TL215.B82A46 2012   j629.222'2   C2012-902287-X

Library of Congress Cataloging-in-Publication Data

CIP available at Library of Congress

Crabtree Publishing Company

www.crabtreebooks.com   1-800-387-7650

Printed in the U.S.A./052012/FA20120413

Published in Canada
Crabtree Publishing
616 Welland Ave.
St. Catharines, Ontario
L2M 5V6

Published in the United States
Crabtree Publishing
PMB 59051
350 Fifth Avenue, 59th Floor
New York, New York 10118

Published in the United Kingdom
Crabtree Publishing
Maritime House
Basin Road North, Hove
BN41 1WR

Published in Australia
Crabtree Publishing
3 Charles Street
Coburg North
VIC 3058

⟩ Contents

Chapter 1
⟫ The Art of the Automobile ⟫⟫⟫

The Bugatti name has always been associated with legendary sports cars. The brand's founder, Italian-born Ettore Bugatti, built less than 10,000 cars between 1910 and 1939, but since then the brand has become hugely successful. Today, Bugattis are among the most sought-after cars in the world.

Luxury and elegance

From the very start of his career, Ettore Bugatti's vision was to produce vehicles that combined luxury, elegance, and style with extraordinary design and engineering. In short, the founder's passion for art and automobiles led him to create one of the most memorable car brands the world has ever seen.

The Bugatti brand

The Bugatti legacy began in the early 1900s, when Ettore and his son Jean began to build cars with the perfect combination of art and technology. Since then, Bugatti has produced some of the most successful racing cars in the world—and also some of the most beautiful and expensive.

Bugatti's home

Ettore Bugatti was born in Milan, Italy, but he spent much of his life on the other side of the Alps in the region of Alsace, which is in the northeastern part of France.

In 1909, the small French village of Molsheim became a part of automotive history. Ettore Bugatti took up residence in the village and began making automobiles there in a former dyeing factory.

The Bugatti brand continues to be associated with wealth and status all over the world.

How much?

Ettore Bugatti built his first cars in 1910. Other auto manufacturers producing cars around this time included Alfa Romeo, Fiat, Ferrari, Porsche, and Ford. These car manufacturers are still producing some of the world's most expensive and *exotic* sports cars. Depending on the model and the country in which they are produced, these amazing vehicles can cost up to US$2 million.

Unique Bugattis

The Bugatti brand is known for the beauty of its designs and for producing some of the fastest, most exclusive cars of all time. Bugatti has a reputation for advanced engineering. It became the first manufacturer to design racing cars as an entire concept—the **chassis** and body were not designed separately, they were created together.

Rise and fall

Every car Bugatti created carried an unforgettable, individual stamp—from the Type 13 of the pre-World War I era to the fabulous Royale. The outbreak of World War II, however, led to the company's untimely decline. During the war, the factory in Molsheim was damaged and Bugatti lost control of the property. After the war, the company had planned to release a special 375-cc (0.4 liter) **supercharged** comeback car, but this was canceled when Ettore Bugatti died in August 1947. The company faced financial difficulties, and was only able to release one more model in the 1950s before closing down.

Artistic influences

Ettore Bugatti's father, Carlo, was a big influence on the way Ettore created his cars. Carlo studied art at the Brera Academy in Milan and the Académie des Beaux Arts in Paris. Then, he worked with ceramics, silverware, and textiles and became a skilled artist and furniture designer. Ettore's younger brother, Rembrandt, was also graced with artistic abilities. He was a talented sculptor.

New lease on life

In 1998, Volkswagen AG decided to bring new life to the legendary Bugatti brand. The company bought all trademark rights to the name and began to plan Bugatti's revival. One year later, Bugatti Automobile S.A.S. was founded in Molsheim, as a **subsidiary** of Volkswagen France. Bugatti is now owned by the Volkswagen Group, which has revived it as a builder of limited edition super cars. VW also owns the luxury car brands of Lamborghini, Bentley, and Audi.

Since taking over the Bugatti name in 1998, Volkswagen has remained true to the brand's tradition of luxury, both inside and out.

The Royale was produced in 1927, and showed the classic elegant styling for which Bugatti had already become famous.

Exclusive and expensive

Today, more than ever before, Bugattis appeal to musicians, actors, and other celebrities because of their beauty and elegance. In 2008, music **executive** and TV star Simon Cowell was seen zipping around Los Angeles in a Bugatti Veyron—one of the world's fastest and most expensive street-legal cars. With more than 1,000 **horsepower (hp)**, Cowell's superstar car has a top speed of 253 mph (408 km/h).

Elite owners

In 2010, Beyoncé Knowles gave her husband, superstar rapper Jay-Z, a US$2 million Bugatti Veyron Grand Sport as a birthday present to add to his huge collection of super cars. Beyoncé had to order the Bugatti a full year in advance. Actor Tom Cruise

and football quarterback Tom Brady are also Bugatti owners. Cruise, one of the wealthiest people in Hollywood, arrived at the premiere of *Mission Impossible 3* in a black and charcoal Bugatti Veyron. The 71-year-old fashion designer Ralph Lauren has also been seen driving around Colorado in a black-on-black Bugatti Veyron. A well-known collector of automobiles, Lauren has more than 70 rare and beautifully designed cars.

■■➡
The super fast Bugatti Veyron is very popular among celebrities, who love its style and power.

The stylized initials of the brand's founder, Ettore Bugatti, have adorned each model since 1909.

Bugatti logo

The elegant, individual, and artistic character of Bugatti automobiles is reflected in the brand's logo. The small pearl-shaped dots that surround the Bugatti name are in stark contrast to the solid white letters with two background colors: black and red. The elegant logo design tells all who see it that Bugatti actually goes beyond engineering and technology.

Chapter 2

The Early Years ≫≫≫

Ettore Bugatti was born in Milan, Italy, in 1881. His younger brother, Rembrandt, was born four years later. Ettore and Rembrandt both had a flair for art, design, and engineering. However, it was Ettore who excelled as an engineer and became the best-known member of the Bugatti family.

When he began to design cars in the early 1900s, Ettore drew on his love of beautiful, handmade crafts. This is the Type 15.

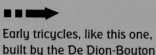 Early tricycles, like this one, built by the De Dion-Bouton company, were often used to pull small carriages with passengers.

Like father, like son

Ettore's father Carlo was a talented artist with strong creative abilities. He devoted himself to building expensive and exclusive furniture. Art critics and historians sometimes classify his work as part of the Arts and Crafts movement, which began in Britain. The movement represented a revolt against mass-produced, machine-made items and instead valued handcrafted, one-of-a-kind pieces. Reflecting on his childhood, Ettore once said, "My first ambition was to be a great artist and so earn the right to bear a name distinguished by my father."

Studying art

As a boy, Ettore worked with Carlo in his workshop, learning how to craft with his hands and finding out about different woods and metals. Carlo decided that his son should also attend the Brera Academy in Milan. At the academy, Ettore studied painting, sculpture, and architecture from some

of the best teachers in Italy. At the age of 17, Ettore decided to leave school and become an unpaid **apprentice** at the manufacturing plant of Prinetti & Stucchi, which made sewing machines, bicycles, and motorized vehicles. During his time there, Ettore built his first motorized tricycle, which was driven by De Dion-Bouton engines.

De Dion-Bouton

De Dion-Bouton was a French automobile and railcar manufacturer that operated from 1883 to 1932. Jules-Albert de Dion, Georges Bouton, and his brother-in-law Charles Trepardoux founded the company in 1881. It was the world's largest automobile manufacturer for a time, and its cars were well known for their quality, reliability, and durability.

11

Self-taught

As an apprentice at Prinetti & Stucchi, Ettore did not learn much about car design. This lack of technical training allowed his artistic side to flourish, and he continued to nurture this part of his character. This had a major influence on the way Ettore designed cars when he began producing them under his own name.

Two is better than one

While working as an apprentice, Ettore began to think of ways to improve the performance of his first tricycle. He had the idea of adding a second engine to the bike, on the opposite side of the large, centrally located drive gear. The crankcase on the second engine was mounted back to back with that of the first engine. This way, the engine's **crankshaft** extension could be joined together.

Driver and mechanic

In the early years of automobile racing, cars almost always broke down during races. It was customary for each car to carry both a driver and a mechanic during a race. The driver raced the car and the mechanic made any repairs that were needed throughout the race.

Get set, go!

Ettore entered his two-engined tricycle in the Turin-Asti-Alessandria-Turin race that was held on July 17, 1898. He did not complete the course on this occasion, but had better luck the following year, when he participated in nine Italian racing contests. He was also featured on the front cover of the Italian motoring magazine *L'Automobili*. Ettore's tricycle won the Guastalla-Reggio and Emilia races, as well as the 47-mile (75-km) race from Bologna "Riunione" to Corticella and back.

Ettore continued to develop Prinetti & Stucchi products, studying the different types of engines being used at the time, examining their parts, and trying to determine the cause of any problems. Ettore's determination to build his first car was growing.

AMAZING FACTS

Lancia links

In 1900, Ettore raced against Vincenzo Lancia in the Italian city of Padua. Like Ettore, Vincenzo founded his own car company, Lancia, in 1906. Lancia became a part of the Fiat Group in 1969.

Ettore Bugatti worked at several automakers before setting up on his own in 1909.

This Bugatti prototype was built for the Paris-Madrid race in around 1901.

First car

In 1901, Ettore completed the construction of his first automobile—called the Type 2. This car was a **prototype** that was financed by Count Gulinelli. The Type 2 won a gold medal in the Milan International Exhibition held in May 1901. Ettore made sure the front-mounted, four-cylinder engine was water-cooled. The car had 3,054-cc (3.1 liter) capacity. Eventually, it also acquired a single headlamp and a third gear lever. It could reach speeds of 37 mph (60 km/h).

Panhard Levassor

The French firm of Panhard and Levassor was one of the *pioneers* of the automobile industry. René Panhard and Émile Levassor established the company in 1887, and they were among the first to use front-mounted engines in their vehicles. The company was taken over by Citroën in the 1960s and stopped building cars in 1967. It still makes military vehicles.

Opportunity in Germany

In 1901, Ettore moved to Niederbronn in Alsace, France, to start a job as technical director of De Dietrich's automobile manufacturing plant. Since Ettore was still under 21 years old, his father had to sign the employment contract on his behalf. While working for De Dietrich, Ettore developed new car models and entered numerous races. This provided excellent publicity for his products.

What's your type?

From 1902 to 1904, around 100 Type 3, Type 4, and Type 5 De Dietrich-Bugatti automobiles were produced. These models were all inspired by the Type 2, which was fitted with a 3,054 cc (3.1 liter) inline four-cylinder engine. The mechanics and the look of all these early cars would influence the design of the cars Ettore later produced under his own name.

■ At the beginning of the twentieth century, De Dietrich had a reputation as a maker of fast touring cars, like this one from 1903.

⚑ AMAZING FACTS

Daring to be different

In 1901, following the International Exhibition in Milan, the paper *Gazzetta dello Sport* described Ettore's car as "the sensational novelty of the Exhibition." It called Ettore "the engaging daredevil of Italian motor cycling."

3 JOT

The Type 5

One of the best cars Ettore developed while working at De Dietrich was the Type 5. The prototype was built by Ettore and his friend Emile Mathis, who was the De Dietrich distributor. The Type 5 was also known as "Hermes," and came equipped with a 12.9-liter four-cylinder inline engine delivering up to 45 hp. It also had a four-speed **manual transmission**.

Ettore Bugatti stands next to one of his early models.

16

Moving on

Ettore left De Dietrich in 1904, and his career continued with a string of different positions in automobile development and construction, including two other German carmakers. Ettore gained valuable experience, which paved the way for him to start building cars under his own name.

Coming to Cologne

In 1907, Ettore married Barbara Maria Giuseppina Mascherpa, who was a childhood friend. They went on to have two sons and two daughters together. On September 1, 1907, Ettore signed on with the gas-engine plant Gasmotoren-Fabrik Deutz in Cologne, Germany. This company was founded in 1864 and is still operating today.

AMAZING FACTS

First overhead camshaft

The world's first overhead *camshaft* racing car was the 17-liter, 100-hp Isotta Fraschini Type D. It was designed by Giuseppe Stefanini and raced in the Coppa Florio on September 10, 1905.

Italian competition

Fiat is one of the best-known car-makers today. It was founded in Italy in 1899, just as Ettore Bugatti was starting to design automobiles. Among the members of Fiat's board of directors, Giovanni Agnelli gained recognition for his determination and vision. In 1902, Agnelli became the managing director of the company. By 1914, Fiat was not only Italy's largest car manufacturer, but also one of Europe's mainstream motor manufacturers.

Lucky 10?

In 1908, in the basement of his home in Cologne, Ettore began to develop an extremely lightweight car. This vehicle, which weighed about 700 pounds (320 kg), became known as the Bugatti Type 10. Ettore fitted the two-seater **roadster** with a 1.1-liter inline engine and a four-speed manual transmission.

Bugatti begins

In 1909, Ettore's contract at Deutz ended before it was due to. The company gave him money to make up for ending the contract early. He used the money to lease an abandoned dye works in Molsheim, Alsace. This area would be home to Ettore and his family for nearly 40 years. He had decided that it was time for the production of the Bugatti Type 13 to officially begin. This was one of the first cars to be produced and sold under the Bugatti name.

The prototype Type 10 featured a bathtub-shaped body and had no rear suspension!

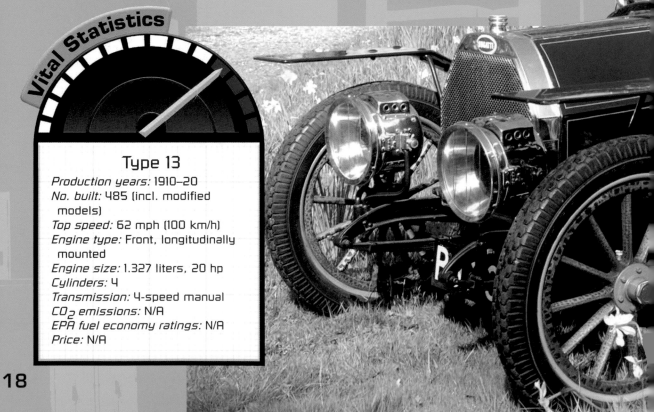

Vital Statistics

Type 13

Production years: 1910–20
No. built: 485 (incl. modified models)
Top speed: 62 mph (100 km/h)
Engine type: Front, longitudinally mounted
Engine size: 1.327 liters, 20 hp
Cylinders: 4
Transmission: 4-speed manual
CO_2 emissions: N/A
EPA fuel economy ratings: N/A
Price: N/A

No frills

When designing the Type 13, Ettore tried to keep it simple and included just the essentials. Despite this, the entire automobile—inside and out—was made with the best materials and **craftsmanship** available at the time. It was this attention to detail that set Bugatti apart from the rest of the industry. During this time, manufacturers and customers alike believed that an expensive car had to be large and luxurious. Bugatti was one of the first manufacturers to ignore such trends.

■ The Type 13 had no frills, but no expense was spared during its construction.

Chapter 3

Making a Name »»»»»»

Ettore Bugatti continued to make a name for himself and his company during the early 1900s. In 1911, he drove his Type 13 in the French Grand Prix at Le Mans, finishing second overall and first in class. His cars continued to perform well on the track, and quickly gained a reputation for being amazing mechanical creations.

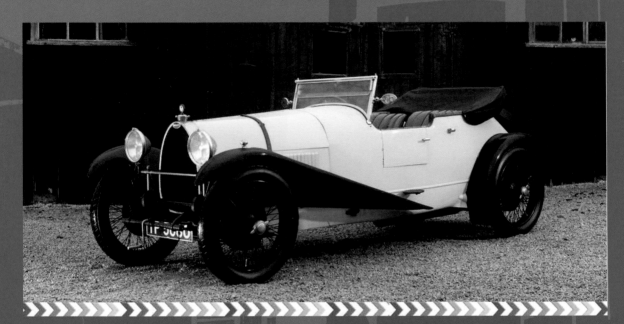

The cars Bugatti built in the early post-war years became known as "Brescias" because of their success at the Brescia Grand Prix.

Buried parts

In 1914, World War I broke out. This halted car production in many countries, as all manufacturing was needed for the war effort. During the war, Ettore returned to Milan, taking some completed Type 13 cars with him. He left the parts for three more cars buried near his factory in France.

After the war, Bugatti returned and prepared five Type 13 cars for racing. They were a great success, winning the first four places at the 1921 Brescia Grand Prix. As a result, Bugatti Type 13 cars are often called the "Brescia" Bugattis. World War I might have had a negative effect on the automobile industry, but by the 1920s, Bugatti orders were pouring in.

Driver Raymond Mays loses a wheel from his Bugatti Brescia during a race in 1924.

Racing success

Ettore saw his opportunity. He decided to take advantage of the racing success of the Brescia by creating the Brescia Tourer. This used the multi-valve Brescia engine, which featured four valves per cylinder. Between 1920 and 1926, 2,000 Brescia Tourers were built, making it the first full-production multi-valve car ever made.

Le Mans

The 24 Hours of Le Mans is an endurance race that has been held annually since 1923 near the town of Le Mans, France. Race teams have to balance speed against the cars' ability to run for 24 hours without any mechanical problems. The endurance of the drivers is also tested, as they frequently have to spend over two hours behind the wheel without a break.

Bugatti Bébé

Before and after World War I, Ettore also worked on a small car that became known as the Type BP1 Bébé. This was a four-cylinder vehicle built for the French car brand Peugeot. Peugeot bought the car from Bugatti in 1911 and made minor changes to the design.

With a revised **grille**, Peugeot was able to sell the car with few other changes to Ettore's original. Peugeot displayed it under its **marque** at the Paris Auto Show in 1912. More than 3,000 Type BP1 Bébés were sold, which made this car the bestselling Bugatti design ever.

The small Type BP1 Bébé had a top speed of 37 mph (60 km/h).

Jean Bugatti inherited his father's (and his grandfather's) artistic abilities, which he applied to his own car designs.

Jean Bugatti

Gianoberto Maria Carlo Bugatti, or Jean as everyone called him, was born on January 15, 1909. He was the third of Ettore's four children. Jean spent the majority of his youth witnessing the first racetrack successes of Bugatti cars. His talent for designing touring and sports cars quickly became obvious. Jean's bodywork designs had a lasting impact on the style of European cars in the 1930s.

Family tragedy

On January 8, 1916, Ettore found out that his brother Rembrandt had committed suicide. Rembrandt had been suffering from money troubles, which were the result of the collapse of the international art market brought on by the war. He could no longer find buyers for his work. He also suffered from depression and was slowly going deaf. Rembrandt was later buried at the Bugatti family vault at Dorlisheim, near Molsheim. Ettore was much saddened by his brother's death, but focused on his work. The post-war years were a boom time for Bugatti.

Winning streak

After the war, Ettore moved his family back to Molsheim, which was now a French territory. He reopened his plant at its original location. There, he continued to build light, elegant sports cars that won him victories at Le Mans in 1920 and Brescia the following year— and three more times after that. Thus began a winning streak that lasted until 1925 and claimed over 400 victories.

The "Cigar"

In 1922, Ettore equipped the Type 29/30 racecar with eight cylinders. It had **hydraulic** brakes and a long, thin chassis. Nicknamed "the Cigar" because of this chassis, the car made its debut in the ACF Grand Prix, where it took second place.

Bugatti (car No. 5) competes in the French Grand Prix in Strasbourg, in 1922.

Streamlining

During the 1920s and 1930s, carmakers began to discover the benefits of *streamlined* cars. These vehicles were designed to have the least wind resistance, or drag. Drag is a force that opposes the motion of a moving car or other object. A streamlined shape produces less drag. Less drag means that the cars can reach higher speeds while keeping control on the road and better gas mileage.

Inside the Cigar

The Type 29/30 had two blocks of four cylinders, and featured three valves per cylinder—two intake and one exhaust. Mounted vertically in the head, the valves were set in motion by one overhead camshaft. Whereas the original three-liter engine used nine bearings to support the crankshaft, the new two-liter had just three. A streamlined version of the Type 30, known as "the Tank," was built for the 1923 French Grand Prix, where it came third.

■ The Type 30 was an eight-cylinder, two-liter beast, with the same long wheelbase chassis as the Type 29/30.

Roads and races

In 1924, Ettore unveiled his newest model—the two-liter Type 35. This car had a finely proportioned body and aluminum wheels with eight spokes. These features showed off Ettore's artistic talents, and the car's design won him respect throughout the motoring world. It also made its mark on the racetrack, where it won many races.

A later version of this car, the T35 TC or T35B, came equipped with a 2.3-liter engine, which gave it even more speed. The Bugatti Type 35 models were the only cars in the 1920s to be designed both for the road and the racetrack.

The Type 35 was built for racing. Today, owners still enjoy putting these cars from the 1920s through their paces.

More models

Ettore designed the Type 35 to be produced in relatively large numbers, and more than 300 models were built between 1924 and 1931. The Type 35 was the first racecar to have its bodywork deliberately styled in a way that had previously been reserved for the road cars of the day.

Radical radiator

The Type 35 had a distinctive, gently curved horseshoe-shaped radiator, which was considered to be one of the most beautiful ever fitted to a racecar. This radiator became a classic feature of Bugattis, and appeared on every

One of the most notable features of the Type 35 was its horseshoe-shaped radiator.

Molsheim car—in one form or another—from that point o. The Type 35 was even delivered to the United States. The stylist and designer of General Motors, Henry C. Haga, owned a model.

Bartolomeo Costantini

Costantini was one of Ettore Bugatti's closest friends. At the end of the war, Costantini joined Fiat, where he met the talented designer Giulio Cappa, who was working on a Bugatti. After racing a Bugatti in the Poggio de Berceto mountain race, Costantini became a member of the Bugatti racing team. He won the Targa Florio twice, and in 1926, he took over from Ettore as Bugatti's racing manager.

Really Royale

In 1926, Bugatti built the Bugatti Royale, also known as the Type 41—one of the most luxurious cars ever made. It had a **wheelbase** of 14 feet (4.3 m) and an overall length of 21 feet (6.4 m). The vehicle weighed 7,000 pounds (3,175 kg), and had a 12.8-liter straight-8 engine. When compared to newer vehicles, the Bugatti is about ten percent longer than a Ford Super Duty F-450 truck, and weighs about the same.

Elephant mascot

A sculpture of a rearing elephant adorned some of the Type 41 Royales. Ettore's brother Rembrandt presented him with the sculpture with the initials "EB" on its base in the early 1900s. Ettore commissioned a small batch of sculptures and some of the Royales were fitted with it. It was meant to represent the Royale's size, strength, and dependability.

Vital Statistics

Type 41 Royale

Production years: 1926–33
No. built: 6
Top speed: 100 mph (160 km/h)
Engine type: Front, longitudinally mounted
Engine size: 12.8 liters, 300 hp
Cylinders: 8
Transmission: 3-speed manual
CO_2 emissions: N/A
EPA fuel economy ratings: N/A
Price: N/A

Three of the six Bugatti Type 41 Royales. This luxurious automobile proved too costly even for the royals it was named for.

Too pricey

Ettore Bugatti wanted the Type 41 Royale, to look much like a Rolls-Royce. He had plans to build only 25 of the Bugatti Royale, and hoped to sell them to members of Europe's royal families. But even wealthy royals were not able to purchase these overpriced cars during the Great Depression (a severe worldwide economic depression that began in most countries in about 1929 and lasted into the early 1940s). Out of the six Royales he made, Bugatti only sold three. The Bugatti Royale is still considered the longest—and one of the rarest—cars in the world.

Chapter 4
Big Changes for Bugatti ≫ ≫≫≫

The 1920s were golden years for Bugatti, but there followed a decade of change. In 1932, Ettore was 51 years old and was beginning to lose interest in his cars. His eldest son, Jean, became more involved in managing the company, while Ettore focused on railcar manufacturing.

Autorails for order

During the difficult years of the Great Depression, Ettore won a contract to build a new high-speed train for the French government.

In the early 1930s, Ettore began producing motorized railcars. He designed a railcar that was capable of reaching 124 mph (200 km/h). The heart of the design was the 12.5-liter, eight-cylinder engine. This was the same engine that powered the magnificent Bugatti Type 41 Royale. There was a total of four engines in one railcar.

■■▶

This poster advertises the speedy Bugatti railcar from the 1930s.

PARIS-VICHY
3 H.49

E.A. Schefer

AUTOMOTRICE RAPIDE BUGATTI

PARIS	:	15ʰ45		CLERMONT-Fᴰ	:	7ʰ50
VICHY	:	19ʰ34	PLM	VICHY	:	8ʰ28
CLERMONT-Fᴰ	:	20ʰ15		PARIS	:	12ʰ26

SAUF DIMANCHES & FÊTES

IMP.CHAIX..PARIS..5-35.

30

Order up!

The first 38-passenger railcar was tested in Alsace in 1933. Very soon, it began carrying passengers between Paris and Deauville. The second one was ready in February 1934, and two more went to the French State Railways before the end of the year, with a new order for five railcars to be built in 1935.

At the same time, the Paris-Lyon-Mediterranean Railway ordered a batch of three, and the Alsace-Lorraine Railway ordered two. From 1933 through 1939, 88 Bugatti railcars were built. Standard railcars had 48 or 62 seats. Their service lasted until 1958.

The Great Depression

The Great Depression was the longest, most widespread, and deepest recession of the twentieth century. Personal income, tax revenue, profits, and prices dropped, while international trade also dropped by more than 50 percent. Unemployment rates rose to 33 percent in the United States. Construction stopped in many countries. Farming and rural areas also suffered as crop prices fell by about 60 percent. In many countries, the negative effects of the Great Depression lasted until the beginning of World War II.

There were 40 Bugatti Type 40A cars, all of them built during 1930 – the first year of the Depression.

Type 57

In 1934, Ettore began production of the Bugatti Type 57. This was a touring car with a 3.3-liter engine and a top speed of 95 mph (153 km/h). The Type 57S/SC is one of the best-known Bugatti cars. The letter S stood for "surbaissé," which means "lowered," although some people believed it stood for "sport." The C stood for "compressor." It had a V-shaped dip at the bottom of the radiator, and mesh grilles on either side of the engine compartment.

■
▼ The Type 57 was the first car that was personally styled by Jean Bugatti, and was an entirely new design.

Type 57SC Atlantic

Production years: 1934–40
No. built: 3
Top speed: 124 mph (200 km/h)
Engine type: Front, longitudinal, supercharged
Engine size: 3.3 liters, 210 hp
Cylinders: 8
Transmission: 4-speed manual
CO_2 emissions: N/A
EPA fuel economy ratings: N/A
Price: N/A

Striking out

The year 1936 changed Ettore Bugatti's world and the Bugatti brand forever. His workers at Molsheim decided to go on strike to try to win better pay and working conditions. Ettore, who had always paid his employees above-average wages and provided social benefits, felt personally insulted by the strike.

The company was still facing financial strain from the Great Depression, and as production at Molsheim ground to a halt, debt quickly began to mount. Ettore distanced himself from his employees, preferring to work almost exclusively from his Paris office. He left management of the Molsheim plant to Jean.

Later variations of the Type 57 included the Atlantic and the Atalante. This is the Type 57S Atalante.

Great garage find

In 2009, a Bugatti Type 57S Atalante—one of only 17 models produced—was discovered in a garage in the U.K. after gathering dust for almost 50 years. It is estimated to be worth over US$4 million! The car was originally owned by the first president of the British Racing Drivers' Club, Earl Howe. Through a series of sales, the automobile ended up in the hands of a doctor named Harold Carr. It was parked in a private garage in 1960 and has not been on the road since.

Victory at Le Mans

In 1937, drivers Jean Pierre Wimille and Robert Benoist won the 24 Hours of Le Mans race in a Model 57G Tank. Ettore and Jean had built this as a road car, but they could not resist proving it on the racetrack. In 1939, Wimille and Pierre Veyron—with only one vehicle at their disposal—drove a Tank to victory once again at Le Mans.

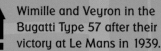
Wimille and Veyron in the Bugatti Type 57 after their victory at Le Mans in 1939.

Pierre Veyron

Pierre Veyron studied engineering before becoming a famous racecar driver in the 1930s. He won his first victory driving a Bugatti Type 37A in the 1930 Geneva Grand Prix, and was offered a job with the Bugatti construction team in 1932. In this role, Veyron both developed and tested the cars, but he still indulged his love of racing and won several races in the Bugatti Type 51A. The Bugatti Veyron is named after him.

The Type 64

At the same time as the Tank was winning at Le Mans, Bugatti was working on the next model—the Type 64. This was intended to be ready for the 1940 racing season.

It was powered by a Type 57 engine with quieter chain-driven camshafts and a standardized gearbox. It kept the Type 57's rigid front axle and **suspension**, and had a rather outdated 3.3-liter fixed head straight-8 engine. Ettore would not let Jean include independently sprung front wheels on the Type 64.

■ The Tank got its nickname from its fully enclosed bodywork, which resembled a tank.

Another tragedy

The 1939 success at Le Mans was the last big win for Bugatti. On August 11, 1939, Jean was killed during a test drive in the same car that had won at Le Mans only weeks before. Driving at more than 124 miles per hour (200 km/h), Jean swerved to avoid a cyclist coming out of a country lane. He lost control of the car, hit a tree, and died on the spot. Ettore was devastated.

▣ AMAZING FACTS

Racing danger

There were no safety features such as seatbelts in cars back in the 1930s, and racing drivers did not wear helmets. Some racecars were open-topped, too, so it was easy to be injured if something went wrong in a race.

The impressive château at Molsheim that Ettore bought in the 1920s.

A new racer

Less than a month after Jean's death, World War II broke out and the Bugatti production facilities were temporarily moved to Bordeaux in France. With the help of his designers, Noel Domboy and Antoine Pichetto, Ettore spent the war years planning a new four-cylinder racing car named the Type 73C. This was to have a supercharged 1500-cc (1.5 liter) 16-valve engine with twin camshafts. By 1944, Ettore's plans for production were in place and further details were released when the war ended the following year.

Château Saint Jean

In the late 1920s, Ettore Bugatti bought a French château in Molsheim, next to the Bugatti manufacturing plant. Although the family never lived in the castle, it perfectly reflected the luxury and elegance of Bugatti's cars, and this nineteenth-century castle was the focal point of the Bugatti brand until World War II. When the plant closed during the war, the castle was abandoned and the family never returned to it.

Get low

Ettore derived the Type 73C's ultra-low racing chassis from the prewar 4.7-liter Type 59/50 B racecar. The engine was all-**alloy** and had detachable wet cylinder liners, a detachable head—a first for Bugatti—and a five-bearing crankshaft. The car also had a four-speed, all **synchromesh** gearbox. In total, the car weighed less than 1,323 pounds (600 kg).

■
■ Several Type 73 prototypes were
↓ built, including the 73A, which was
intended to be available in two-
or four-seater models.

Coming up short

Just 20 73Cs were planned, at a price of 500,000 French francs each. Five were to be delivered in April 1946, with five more during each of the next three months. Fifteen French racing drivers had already put down deposits of 25,000 francs, and English readers of *The Motor* magazine were invited to order the remaining five. However, this timetable proved difficult to achieve. Money was tight after the war, and the materials required for car manufacturing were all in extremely short supply. Several orders were canceled.

The death of Ettore

Eventually a batch of five complete sets of parts for the Type 73C was produced, and an artist's impression of a planned **aerodynamic** sports **sedan** appeared in several motor magazines. However, Ettore's health was rapidly declining and on August 21, 1947, at the age of 66, he died of a lung infection in a military hospital in Paris.

Without Ettore's influence and attention, the Type 73C project slowly ground to a halt. The unfinished cars were dismantled, all their parts were put into storage at Molsheim, and the customers' deposits were returned.

The Belgian Bugatti dealer

The Type 73C parts remained stored at Molsheim for several years. In late 1960, a Belgian Bugatti dealer named Jean de Dobbeleer acquired one set of Type 73C parts. He assembled and fitted a typical Bugatti radiator shell based on a 1945 Type 73C drawing by Antoine Pichetto. After selling the finished car to a Frenchman, de Dobbeleer returned to Molsheim in 1961 and bought the parts for another Type 73C.

AMAZING FACTS

Ettore's legacy

Ettore was buried in Dorlisheim, near Molsheim, in the Bugatti family plot. His legacy lives on in the great many cars that still exist, most of which command the highest prices in the world.

Fully restored

The Type 73C car was purchased in 1969 by Eric Richardson, the leading American Bugatti authority of his day. It was then passed to Tom Wheatcroft, who was in the process of both buying and assembling what was to become his famous Donington Collection of Grand Prix racecars. The Type 73C was fully restored in the Donington workshops.

Tom Wheatcroft built a racetrack in Leicestershire, England, which still hosts races for vintage cars.

Bugatti Owners' Club

The Bugatti Owners' Club is the oldest Bugatti club in the world. It was formed in 1929, and Jean Bugatti joined the following year, attending its dinners from 1937 to 1939. The club operates the Prescott Speed Hill Climb, a hill climb course in Gloucestershire, England. The fastest modern-day racing cars can complete the course in an exciting 36 seconds, and visitors and competitors alike can enjoy exhilarating races and processions of vintage cars up the hill.

A Bugatti takes a corner at the famous Prescott Speed Hill Climb race.

Further improvements

The Type 73C was fitted with a copy of the second of Pichetto's 1945 73C body designs. This one featured a hooded radiator grille that was fashionable in the years just before and after the war.

In 1994, Wheatcroft sold his Type 73C Bugatti to a Mexican named Alberto Lenz. Lenz in turn sold the car to its current owner in 2002. He made a number of improvements, including fitting the car with piano-wire wheels and hubs by Crosthwaite & Gardiner. He added **cycle wings** to make the car street-legal.

Last racing car

Most critics and car enthusiasts believe that the Type 73C Bugatti was no more than an undeveloped factory prototype, which never got to show its true potential or compete in a motor race. The car does

Paris Auto Show

One version of the Type 73 appeared—without its engine—at the Paris Auto Show in 1947. This show, sometimes known as the Paris Motor Show, is an exhibition held every two years in Paris, France, usually sometime in October. It is one of the most important auto shows for debuting new *production cars* and *concept cars*. Started in 1898 by Albert de Dion, it was the first official auto show in the world.

A Bugatti on display at the Paris Auto Show in 1947.

have one claim to fame, however, which it will retain for all time. It was the very last racer designed by perhaps the greatest and certainly the most successful racecar designer ever.

Ferrari

Italian-born Enzo Ferrari began to produce cars in 1947, just two years after the end of World War II. Ferrari modeled his own company after Bugatti. With their sleek designs and unmatched speed, Ferraris epitomize style and elegance, and they have reigned over the European racing scene for over 70 years. Ferrari has had countless Formula 1, Grand Prix, and 24 Hours of Le Mans racing victories. In fact, Ferraris have been in more Formula 1 races than any other car ever made!

Chapter 5
A New Bugatti ⟫ ⟫ ⟫ ⟫ ⟫ ⟫ ⟫

After World War II, Jean's younger brother Roland tried to take over the Bugatti business. However, without Ettore and Jean, the company never caught up with the latest automotive developments and soon went out of business. The brand of exquisite automobiles Ettore Bugatti developed from the ground up ceased to exist for many years. Later, though, it was revived by Volkswagen, which rebuilt the old Molsheim facilities.

A family divided

At the time of his death, Ettore Bugatti had five living children. L'Ébé was his eldest daughter, and his second daughter was Lidia. Roland was Jean's younger brother. Ettore also had two children from a second marriage to 25-year-old Geneviève Marguerite Delcuze.

Thérésa was born in 1942 and Michel was born in 1945. Ettore left Geneviève a 50 percent stake in the Bugatti business, but Ettore's family soon divided themselves into two opposing sides. The children from Ettore's first marriage were on one side, and his second wife and her children were on the other.

Ettore Bugatti behind the wheel, with his sons Jean and Roland.

The Type 101

On March 2, 1951, *The Autocar* magazine reported that "two new models in production before the end of the year is the latest hope of the Bugatti company." One new model was the Type 101, eight of which were produced. Its 3.3-liter 8-cylinder inline engine was based on the Type 57 engine and delivered 135 hp. Its chassis was also developed as a natural progression of the one used in the Type 57. The Type 101 was displayed at the 1951 Paris Auto Show, but no orders came in.

 Designed as a luxurious roadster, the Type 101 was launched by Bugatti in 1951.

Type 251

Among the final revival of the original Bugatti was the Type 251, which was completed in 1955 and was powered by a new 2.5-liter straight-8 engine. One unique feature was that the engine was mounted transversely, behind the driver.

The Type 251 was entered in the 1956 French Grand Prix, but only lasted 18 laps. This was the last Bugatti Grand Prix car to be built at Molsheim.

Testing failure

It was much the same story with the 1.5-liter, four-cylinder Type 252 sports car. A prototype was built, but it was a failure during testing. The Type 252 never really got beyond the early stages, and just one model can now be found in the Cité de l'Automobile museum in Mulhouse, France.

The Type 251 was designed by Gioacchino Colombo of Ferrari.

Bugatti owners' clubs allow people to show off and share information about their Bugattis.

Saying goodbye

By the early 1960s, the Bugatti factory was struggling financially. In July 1963, the Spanish automotive and engineering firm Hispano-Suiza took over and the Bugatti family said farewell to the workers at Molsheim. The purchase meant that there were no links between the Bugatti family and Molsheim for the first time in over 50 years. However, in 1968, Hispano-Suiza was itself taken over by Société Nationale d'Études et de Construction de Moteurs d'Aviation (SNECMA), a world-class manufacturer of aircraft and rocket engines.

Join the club

The American Bugatti Club was founded in California, in 1960, to encourage interest in Bugattis and provide a network in the United States for members to learn more about each other and their cars. The club encourages members to gather at events, share experiences, and enjoy using their Bugattis in races, hill climbs, and rallies across the country.

New company, new car

Bugatti finally made a real comeback at the end of 1987. Italian entrepreneur Romano Artioli acquired the Bugatti name and established Bugatti Automobili S.p.A., with the intention of producing a new Bugatti car. This new vehicle was to be powered by a 3.5-liter V12 engine. It had a projected top speed of 210 mph (338 km/h), which would put it in competition with Jaguar, BMW, and Aston Martin. The engine would be rear-mounted and the new Bugatti would be a four-wheel-drive car.

The EB 110 was equipped with lifting scissor doors and a glass engine cover that provided a full view of the V12 engine.

AMAZING FACTS

Fit for a champion

The most famous Bugatti EB 110 owner was probably the racecar driver Michael Schumacher. Schumacher is a seven-time Formula 1 world champion.

Schlumpf brothers

The Schlumpf brothers, Hans and Fritz, built up an extensive collection of Bugattis in Mulhouse, France. In the early 1960s, they bought 18 historic cars before the Bugatti company was taken over. The collection was later bought by the French government and turned into the Cité de l'Automobile. The museum is one of the most popular tourist attractions in France.

Links to the past

A new factory was also built in Campogalliano, about six miles (ten km) from Modena, Italy. The official opening of the factory took place on September 15, 1990. A link between Molsheim and the new factory was created when a flame was lit from the old foundry at the Alsace plant and carried to Campogalliano in a 1934 Type 57. Approximately 1,200 guests, including Ettore's son Michel Bugatti, attended the opening ceremony.

Bugatti EB 110

On September 15, 1991—on what would have been Ettore Bugatti's 110th birthday—the EB 110 was introduced in Versailles and in front of the Grande Arche de La Défense in Paris. The 12-cylinder car boasted four **turbochargers**, four-wheel drive, and approximately 560 hp. It had a 3.5-liter engine and could reach 62 mph (100 km/h) in just 3.4 seconds. About 150 units of this model were manufactured.

An EB 110 being built at the Campogalliano factory near Modena, Italy.

Revival

Just over ten years later, in 1998, the Bugatti brand was bought out by Volkswagen AG. Almost immediately, it launched a new Bugatti—putting the prototype on display at the Paris Auto Show. The following year, Volkswagen established the new Bugatti Automobile S.A.S. back in Molsheim.

Bugatti EB 118

The first Bugatti prototype was the Bugatti EB 118, which was a creation of the renowned Italian design company ItalDesign. Volkswagen hired ItalDesign to dream up a new luxury car for the Bugatti marque.

The EB 118 prototype boasted a computerized dashboard.

ItalDesign

ItalDesign S.p.A. is a car design and engineering company based in Moncalieri, Italy. It was founded in 1968 by Giorgetto Giugiaro and Aldo Mantovani as Studi Italiani Realizzazione Prototipi S.p.A. The company is best known for its automobile design work, but also offers project management, styling, packaging, engineering, modeling, and testing services to manufacturers around the world.

Italian style

The design of the EB 118 was partly influenced by the swooping lines of the Bugatti Type 57 Atlantic from 1934. The EB 118 was a two-door **coupe** featuring a 6.3-liter turbocharged 18-cylinder engine. It had permanent all-wheel drive and a lightweight aluminum frame.

■
■
↓ The EB 118 at its launch at the 1998 Paris Motor Show.

Birth of the EB 218

The EB 118 was followed by another ItalDesign creation. The powerful and sporty Bugatti EB 218 was a four-door limousine. It was presented at the Geneva Motor Show in 1999.

The EB 218 had a 9.8-foot (3-m) wheelbase and featured a longitudinal groove that was rather like the one on the Bugatti Atlantic. Power came from an 18-cylinder, 6.3-liter engine.

Power and elegance

Technology and design came together in the EB 218. The 18-cylinder engine was one of the first of its kind to be used in a passenger vehicle. The **spoiler** extended automatically from the lower edge of the back window. The smooth lines of the body told buyers this was a car that was both powerful and elegant.

Vital Statistics

EB 218

Production years: 1999
No. built: N/A
Top speed: 155 mph (249 km/h)
Engine type: Front, longitudinally mounted
Engine size: 6.3 liters
Cylinders: 18
Transmission: 5-speed automatic
CO_2 emissions: N/A
EPA fuel economy ratings: N/A
Price: N/A

Bugatti 18.3 Chiron

At the International Automobile Exhibition in Frankfurt in the fall of 1999, Volkswagen introduced the Bugatti 18.3 Chiron. This concept sports car was designed by Giorgetto Giugiaro and had the same 18-cylinder engine found in the EB 118 and EB 218 concept cars.

Important design elements included the return of the much-loved curved horseshoe-shaped radiator, inset front lights, and the converging front hood. All these elements were eventually used in the final production model. At high speeds, a retractable rear wing could be deployed.

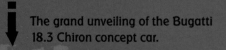

The grand unveiling of the Bugatti 18.3 Chiron concept car.

51

Louis Chiron

The 18.3 Chiron was named after Louis Chiron, a well-known racecar driver. Chiron was born in Monaco in 1899, and was a professional dancer before he discovered his passion for motor racing. After World War I, Chiron went into business with William Charles Grover, opening a car dealership in Nice. It was there that the two men built up a business relationship with Ettore Bugatti. Both Chiron and Grover went on to be successful racecar drivers for the Bugatti team.

Bunches of Bugattis

In 2010, the American Bugatti Club announced the International Bugatti Rally along the Pacific coast of California. Seventy-three Bugattis from all over the world gathered in Monterey, California, on August 16 to begin the rally. It was one of the largest gatherings of Bugatti enthusiasts and cars in the world.

One of the first Bugatti Veyron 16.4s.

Chiron at Bugatti

Chiron joined the Bugatti team in 1928. He was very successful for his new team, winning races all over Europe.
He drove various Bugatti cars, including the Brescia and the Types 30, 35, and 35B. Chiron was particularly successful in the Grand Prix, winning in 1926 at Comminges and also taking the 1927 French Grand Prix. He also won fourth place in the European Grand Prix in England the same year.

After four years, Bugatti no longer featured so prominently in racing programs, but by this time, Chiron had made a name for himself as one of the best drivers of the era.

Louis Chiron and his Bugatti Type 51.

Super sports car

In 2001, Volkswagen decided to start production of a super sports car. This came to be known as the Veyron 16.4. In 2004, after renovation of the Bugatti headquarters at Château Saint Jean was completed and the new assembly studio constructed, Bugatti S.A.S. began manufacturing the first Veyron. The development of the Veyron 16.4 not only breathed new life into the company, but it became one of the key milestones of twenty-first-century carmaking.

Chapter 6

➤ Bugatti Lives On ➤➤➤➤➤➤

Bugatti has certainly come a long way from the modest two-engined tricycle that appeared more than 100 years ago. Today, Bugatti's designers, engineers, and technicians continue to produce some of the most spectacular automobiles in the world—and some of the fastest vehicles of all time.

Bugatti Veyron 16.4

The Bugatti Veyron was first shown at the Tokyo Motor Show in 2004. The 16-cylinder four-wheel drive car has been called the most sophisticated production car ever. It boasts a maximum speed of more than 250 mph (400 km/h). The car goes from 0 to 62 mph (100 km/h) in only 2.5 seconds and actually reaches velocities that would literally lift the car off the ground if it were not for its superb aerodynamics. It is a winning combination of engine technology, lightweight construction, specially developed tires, and the perfect balance between **propulsion** and **downforce**.

Veyron 16.4

Production years: 2005–present
No. built: Built to order
Top speed: 253 mph (407 km/h)
Engine type: Internal combustion engine in a four-bank W configuration
Engine size: 8 liters
Cylinders: 16
Transmission: 7-speed DSG sequential
CO_2 emissions: 596 g/km
EPA fuel economy ratings: 11.2 gallons/62 miles (42.5 l/100 km) (city); 4.3 gal./62 mi (16.2 l/100 km) (highway)
Price: Approx. US$1.7 million

Bugatti Grand Sport

The Bugatti Veyron 16.4 Grand Sport combines design and technology with the beauty of a convertible car. With 16 cylinders, a combined capacity of eight liters, four valves per cylinder, and four turbochargers, the Grand Sport's engine is the most powerful ever to be built into a production vehicle. The Grand Sport's gears shift in milliseconds, allowing for super-fast **acceleration** up to and exceeding 250 mph (400 km/h).

The Grand Sport is a modern-day example of Bugatti's core values of art, form, and technique.

The three Grand Sport special editions, on display at the Dubai Motor Show in November 2011.

Veyron special editions

The Grand Sport not only demonstrates the creativity of the Bugatti brand, but it also fulfills the desire for customized, luxury vehicles in the Middle East and enthralls car enthusiasts from around the world. In terms of colors and materials, the first special-edition model boasted light yellow and black carbon.

The second had blue carbon trimmed with polished aluminum. The third model featured the traditional Bugatti two-tone design, with green carbon fiber and polished aluminum.

Veyron 16.4 Super Sport

Production years: 2010–present
No. built: Built to order
Top speed: 268 mph (431 km/h)
Engine type: 7,993 cc (8 l) quad-turbo
Engine size: 8 liters
Cylinders: 16
Transmission: 7-gear DSG sequential
CO_2 emissions: 867 g/km
EPA fuel economy ratings: 9.8 gal./62 mi. (37.2 l/100 km) (city); 3.9 gal./62 mi. (14.9 l/100 km) (highway)
Price: Approx. US$1.9 million

The Veyron Super Sport is the fastest production car in the world.

Bugatti in Dubai

In November 2011, Bugatti showcased three spectacular special edition models of the legendary Bugatti Veyron 16.4 Grand Sport at the Dubai International Motor Show. This motor show attracts some of the most discerning car enthusiasts and customers in the world. It is the ideal platform for showcasing the world's fastest, most powerful, and most exclusive convertible car.

Bugatti Super Sport

The sportier and more extreme Bugatti Veyron 16.4 Super Sport is the climax of the Veyron series. It is the fastest road-legal production car in the world, with a top speed of 268 mph (431 km/h). It has already been entered into the *Guinness Book of World Records*.

Bugatti blows the bank

A set of new tires for a Bugatti Veyron will cost close to US$40,000. At every fourth tire change, the Veyron's wheels must be stress tested for cracks. The replacement cost for each of these 20-inch (51-cm) wheels can be another US$11,000. A replacement transmission for a Veyron costs just over US$120,000!

Super Sport convertible

The convertible version of the Super Sport made its debut at the 2012 Geneva Motor Show and secured its spot as the fastest convertible in the world. The Super Sport has a 1,200-hp quad-turbocharged eight-liter engine and does 0 to 62 mph (100 km/h) in 2.5 seconds.

All Veyrons are carefully hand-assembled, which makes them unique and desirable – but also expensive!

Manufacturing with a view

Today, Bugatti Veyron models are made in a newly created production site located near the current offices at Château Saint Jean. The outer part of the building is made of aluminum on concrete foundations, with a steel frame. The main building is an oval shape and this, together with its construction materials and huge windows, makes it feel very light and offers beautiful views of the French countryside.

Back to handcrafted

Manufacturing techniques today go back to Bugatti's early traditions of handmade craftsmanship. In the factory, Veyrons are painstakingly put together by hand rather than being assembled by machines. There are three assembly stations, along with separate facilities for testing each vehicle before it is shipped off to its buyer.

Certified Heritage Cars

Recently, Bugatti started the Certified Heritage Cars Program, which guarantees the impeccable condition of all Bugatti vehicles, including the assurance of the highest Bugatti quality standards and the exclusive use of original parts. Specially trained Bugatti technicians inspect vehicles through all their stages, to guarantee their perfect technical condition.

Bugatti Timeline

1881   Ettore Bugatti is born

1899   Ettore takes part in nine races on his twin-engined tricycle

1901   The Type 2 wins gold at the Milan International Exhibition; Ettore starts work for De Dietrich

1902   Work begins on the Type 3

1904   Ettore leaves De Dietrich

1907   Ettore starts work with German company Gasmotoren-Fabrik Deutz

1908   Ettore begins work on the Type 10

1909   Bugatti factory opens in Molsheim, France

1910   The Type 13 is released

1911   Peugeot buys the design for the Bébe from Bugatti

1914   World War I breaks out and car production is halted

1921   Bugatti takes the first four places at the Brescia Grand Prix

1922   Bugatti launches the Type 29/30 racecar, nicknamed "the Cigar"

1924   Launch of the Type 35

1926   Bartolomeo Costantini takes over as Bugatti's race manager; Bugatti produces the Type 41 Royale

1929   The Bugatti Owners' Club is founded; the Great Depression begins

1934   Production begins on the Type 57

1936   A strike at the Molsheim plant causes financial difficulties for Bugatti

1937   The Model 57G Tank wins the 24 Hours of Le Mans

1939   Jean Bugatti is killed during a test drive; World War II breaks out

1947   Ettore Bugatti dies

1951   The Type 101 is launched

1955   The Type 251 is completed

1956   The Type 251 fails at the French Grand Prix, dropping out after 18 laps

1960   The American Bugatti Club is founded in California

1963   Spanish auto manufacturer Hispano-Suiza takes over the Molsheim factory from the Bugatti family

1968   SNECMA takes over from Hispana-Suiza

1987   Romano Artioli buys the Bugatti name

1990   The Campogalliano factory is officially opened

1991   The EB 110 is launched

1998   Volkswagen AG buys the rights to the Bugatti brand and launches the EB 118

1999   Bugatti Automobile S.A.S. is founded in Molsheim; the 18.3 Chiron goes on show

2004   The Veyron 16.4 is unveiled at the Tokyo Motor Show

2011   Three Veyron special edition cars are exhibited at the Dubai Motor Show

2012   The Veyron 16.4 Super Sport becomes the fastest street-legal production car in the world

Further Information

Books

Bugatti Veyron: A Quest for Perfection
by Martin Roach
(Preface Publishing, 2011)

Bugatti (Full Throttle)
by Tracy Maurer
(Rourke Publishing, 2008)

Bugatti: The Man and the Marque
by Jonathan Wood
(Crowood, 2007)

Websites

www.bugatti.com/en/home.html
The official Bugatti website, with information
on the company's history and all its models—
past and present.

www.bugatti.co.uk/
The home page of the famous UK Bugatti
Prescott Speed Hill Climb and the Bugatti
Owners' Club.

Glossary

acceleration A measure of how quickly something speeds up

aerodynamic Describing something with a low amount of drag

alloy A substance consisting of two or more metals or of a metal and a non-metal combined

apprentice Someone who works for an agreed amount of time in exchange for being taught a particular business or trade

camshaft A rod in a car's engine; as the camshaft turns, it pushes the pistons up and down, compressing gas in the engine and powering the car

chassis The strong support structure that connects the engine to the wheels and holds the body to the car

concept cars Vehicles made to show the public a new design or technology

coupe A hard-topped sports car with two doors

craftsmanship Having a great talent for something creative

crankshaft A device in a vehicle's engine that works with the pistons to create motion

cycle wings Parts of a car that are fitted over the wheels to stop mud and spray being thrown in the air

downforce The downward pressure created by the aerodynamics of a car that allows it to travel faster

executive Someone in a governing or management position at a company

exotic Something different or unusual

grille The front screen of a vehicle that usually sits between the headlights

horsepower (hp) The amount of pulling power an engine has based on the number of horses it would take to pull the same load

hydraulic Something that is powered or operated by water

manual transmission A device that a driver must operate to shift a car's gears

marque A brand name

pioneers People who are the first to do something

production cars Cars that are made in large numbers on an assembly line

propulsion Moving something forward

prototype The original or test version of a car, which is later modified and developed into a production car

roadster A two-seater car with a soft-top roof and no rear or side windows; also known as a spyder

sedan A passenger car with four doors and a back seat

spoiler A device added to the back of a car that helps reduce drag

streamlined Something that is designed to have the least resistance to the flow of air

subsidiary A company that is owned and run by another company

supercharged When an air compressor is used for the forced induction of an internal combustion engine

suspension A system of springs that protects the chassis of a car

synchromesh A system for shifting gears that allows them to revolve at the same speed, so that they can be shifted smoothly

turbochargers Gas compressors in the engine that make a vehicle go faster

wheelbase The distance between the front and rear wheels on a car

»» Index

Entries in **bold** indicate pictures